ABC

Snake Book

Jessica Lee Anderson

AO PRESS

Paperback ISBN: 979-8-9899560-1-2

Many thanks to Clint Laidlaw (Clint's Reptiles) for reviewing this book for accuracy!

To Craig Randall and Brian Parkhurst—thanks for your insights and friendship! - JLA

Photo credits—Front Cover: LeMusique, bajongseal324, dominicky, JackBuu (Ball Python), Bob Eastman (Nelson's Milksnake), pumppump (Cobra); Back Cover: sannevdberg (Boa Constrictor); Cover Page: LeMusique, bajongseal324, fastfun23, Life On White (Scaleless Corn Snake); Copyright page: Passion4Nature (Ribbon Snake); p. 3: Nynke van Holten; p. 4: Farinosa; p. 5: Life On White, bennymarty; p. 6: Banu R; p. 7: Jay Pierstorff, rick734; p. 8: NajaShots, cturtletrax; p. 9: DustyFog, Wirestock; p. 10: Yuval Helfman, NNehring; p. 11: Reptiles4All; p. 12: sstaton, p. 13: Murilo Gualda p. 14: David Kenny; p. 15: Shoemcfly; p. 16 bwzenith, Reptiles4All; p. 17: DraganSaponjic; p. 18: Ken Griffiths; p. 19: Mark Kostich, Alatom; p. 20: Deposit Photos; p. 21: Florian Denis; p. 22: Mark Kostich; p. 23 & 24: Ken Griffiths; p. 25: Estellez; p. 26: dndavis, sakhorn38, Kristada Petchuay; p. 27: JohnAudrey p. 28: Ken Griffiths; p. 29: shumba138; p. 30: Life On White (Trans-Pecos Rat Snake), the4Js (Rough Green Snake); p. 31: Jason Ondreicka (Eastern Coral Snake); p. 32: Michael and Ava Anderson

Key:

= non-venomous species

= venomous species

= mildly venomous species (mostly a concern for prey, not humans)

This Book Belongs to:

_____

Eunectes murinus

Bonus: the Green Anaconda is the heaviest snake in the world!

A is for Amazon Tree Boa

Corallus hortulanus

Amazon Tree Boas are slender snakes with good eyesight that are arboreal. This means they live in trees.

B is for Ball Python

Python regius

Ball Pythons come in many different "morphs" or color/pattern varieties. They coil into a ball if they get stressed (which is how they got their name).

C is for Coachwhip

Masticophis flagellum

The Coachwhip is long, slender, and fast! The name comes from the snake's tail that looks like a braided whip.

D is for Desert Kingsnake

Lampropeltis splendida

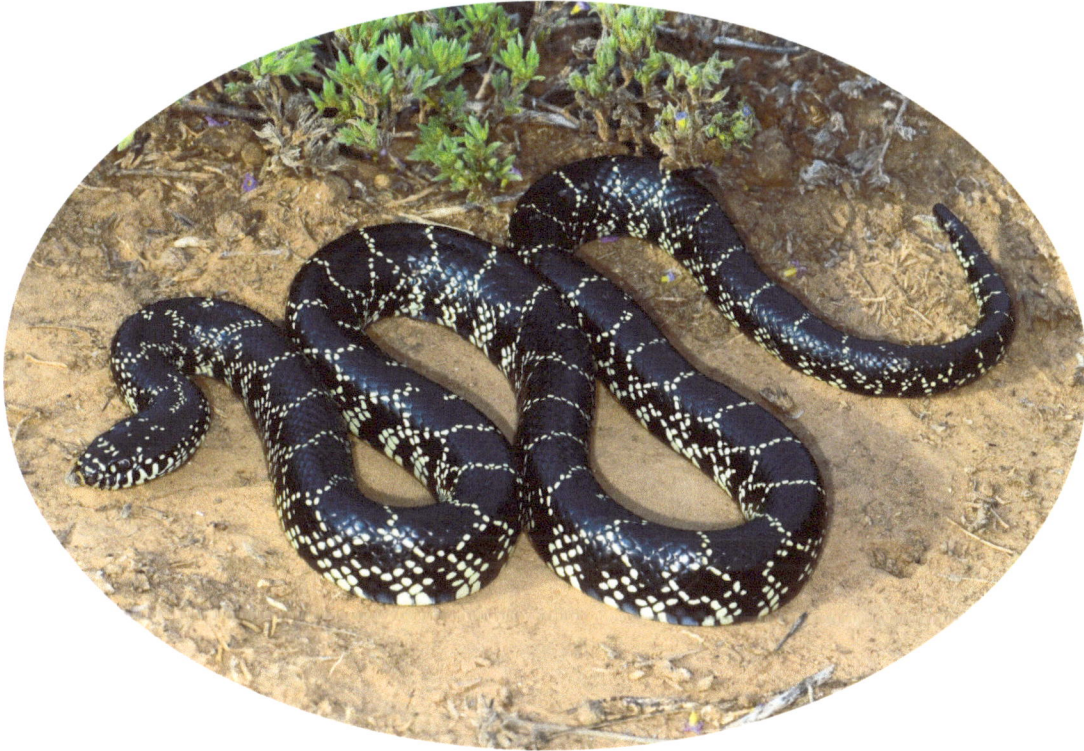

The Desert Kingsnake can safely eat venomous snakes like coral snakes or rattlesnakes. Desert Kingsnakes are immune, or protected, against certain types of venom.

E is for Eastern Hognose

Heterodon platirhinos

The Eastern Hognose has a hog-like snout it uses to dig up dinner. If it senses danger, the Eastern Hognose will puff up or act as if it is dying (which is why they have the nickname "Drama Noodles").

F is for Flying Snake

Chrysopelea paradisi

The Flying Snake is also known as the Paradise Tree Snake or Paradise Flying Snake. This slender snake can glide through the air!

G is for Gopher Snake

Pituophis catenifer

Gopher Snakes are large and powerful. They spend much of their time in underground burrows.

H is for Honduran Milk Snake

Lampropeltis triangulum hondurensis

The Honduran Milk Snake is one of the biggest types of milk snakes. They constrict by wrapping around their prey before swallowing it down.

I is for Indigo

Drymarchon couperi

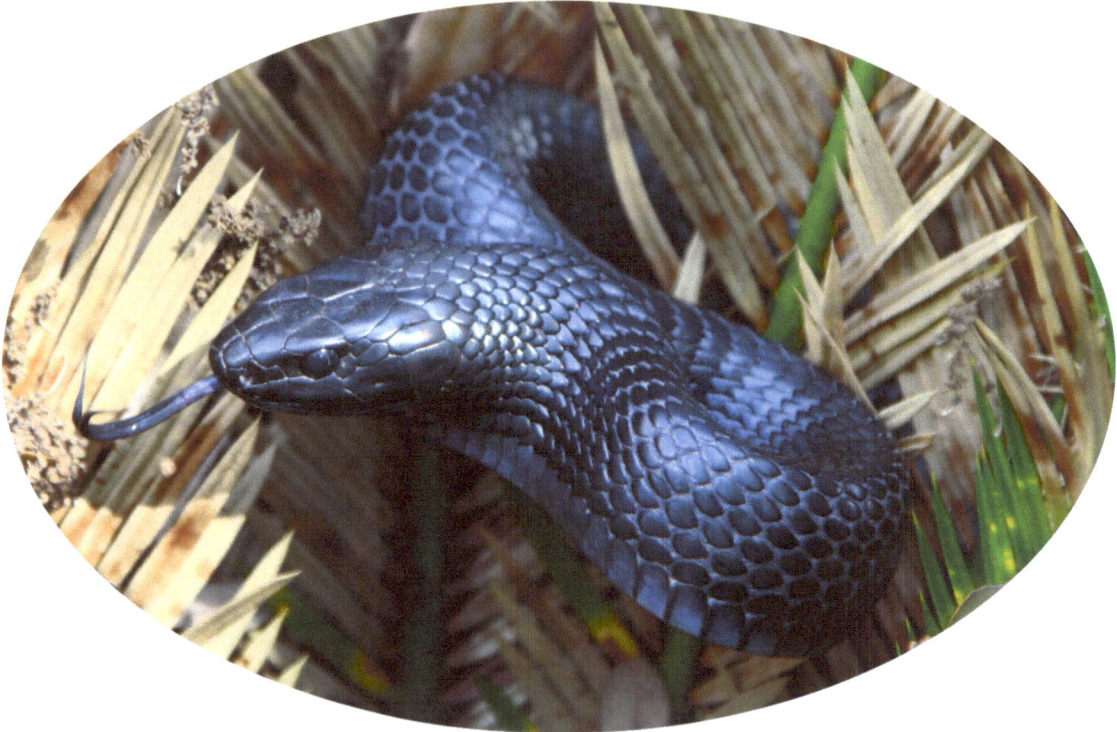

The Indigo, specifically the Eastern Indigo, is one of the longest snakes in the United States. The longest Indigo found was nearly 9 feet long (2.7 meters)!

J is for Jararaca

Bothrops jararaca

The Jararaca is also known as the Yarará. It produces venom that has been used to make medicines to help treat people with heart problems.

K is for Kenyan Sand Boa

Gongylophis (Eryx) colubrinus loveridgei

The Kenyan Sand Boa has a thick, stocky build with a small head and small eyes. Kenyan Sand Boas will burrow in the sand to feel safe and stay cool during the day.

L is for Longnose Snake

Rhinocheilus lecontei

The Longnose Snake, well, has a long nose. These snakes look speckled with cream/yellow, red, and black colors touching—serving as an example as to why the coral snake rhyme is flawed.

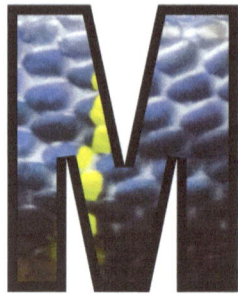

M is for Mangrove Snake

Boiga dendrophila

Mangrove Snakes are nocturnal, meaning they are active at night. Mangrove Snakes are also arboreal, though they are good swimmers as well.

N is for Nose-horned Viper

Vipera ammodytes

The Nose-horned Viper has a single "horn" on its snout. The color patterns will vary if the snake is male or female.

O is for Olive Python

Liasis olivaceus

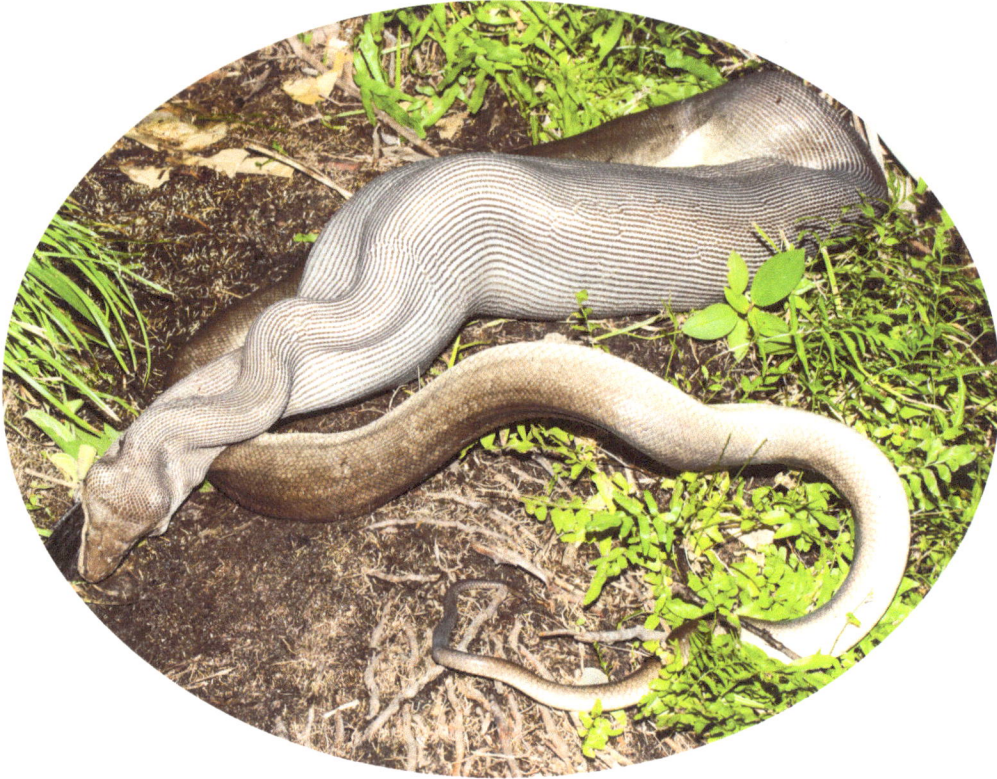

Olive Pythons are some of Australia's biggest pythons! They can eat large animals.

P is for Parrot Snake

Leptophis ahaetulla

The Parrot Snake is also known as the Lora, named for its bright colors. They are slender snakes and mimic vines which helps them to sneak up on prey while hunting.

19

Q is for Queen Snake

Regina septemvittata

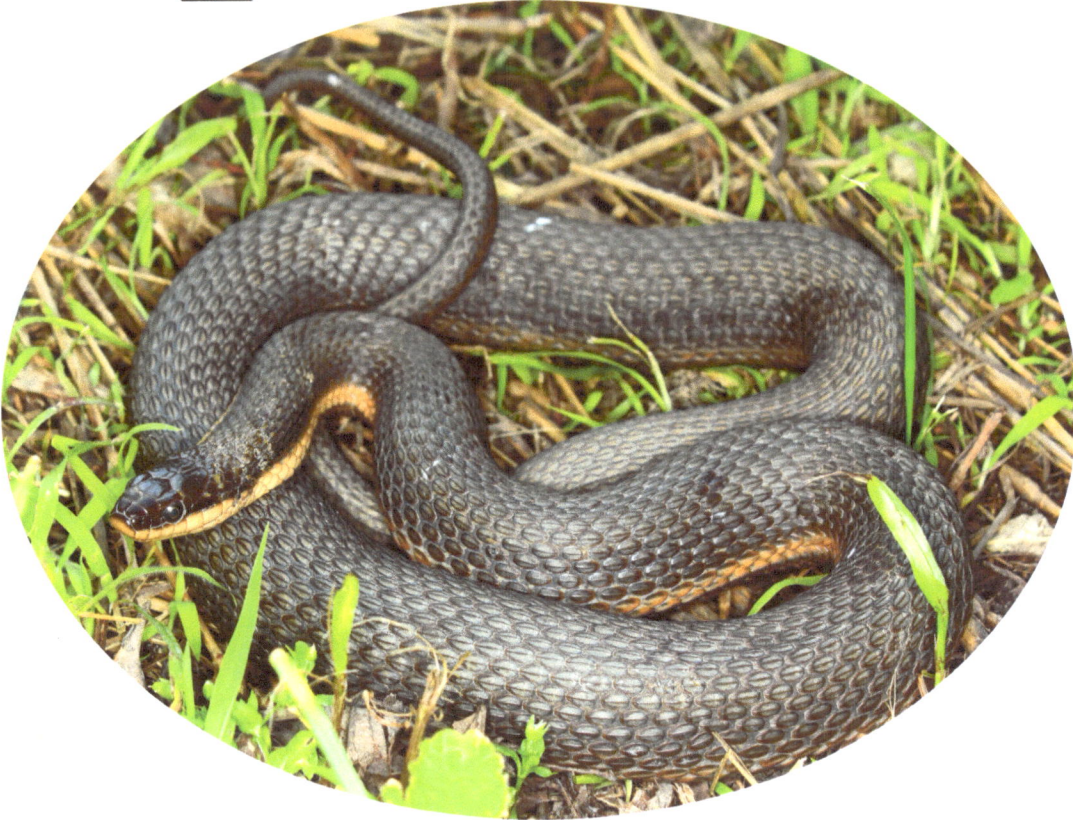

Queen Snakes are non-venomous snakes that live near the water. Like many other water snakes, Queen Snakes give live birth.

R is for Reticulated Python

Malayopython reticulatus

The Reticulated Python is the world's longest snake. Some Reticulated Pythons can be longer than 20 feet (6 meters)—that's as long as a giraffe is tall!

S is for Sidewinder

Crotalus cerastes

Sidewinders are a type of rattlesnake that live in the desert. They get their name because of the way they move across the desert sand.

T is for Taipan

Oxyuranus microlepidotus

The Taipan, specifically the Inland Taipan, is considered by some to be the most venomous snake in the world. They strike lighting-fast, though they are not aggressive.

U is for Urutu

Bothrops alternatus

The Urutu is a type of viper that lives in South America. Their colors and patterns help them to camouflage, meaning they blend into their environment.

V is for Viperine Snake

Natrix maura

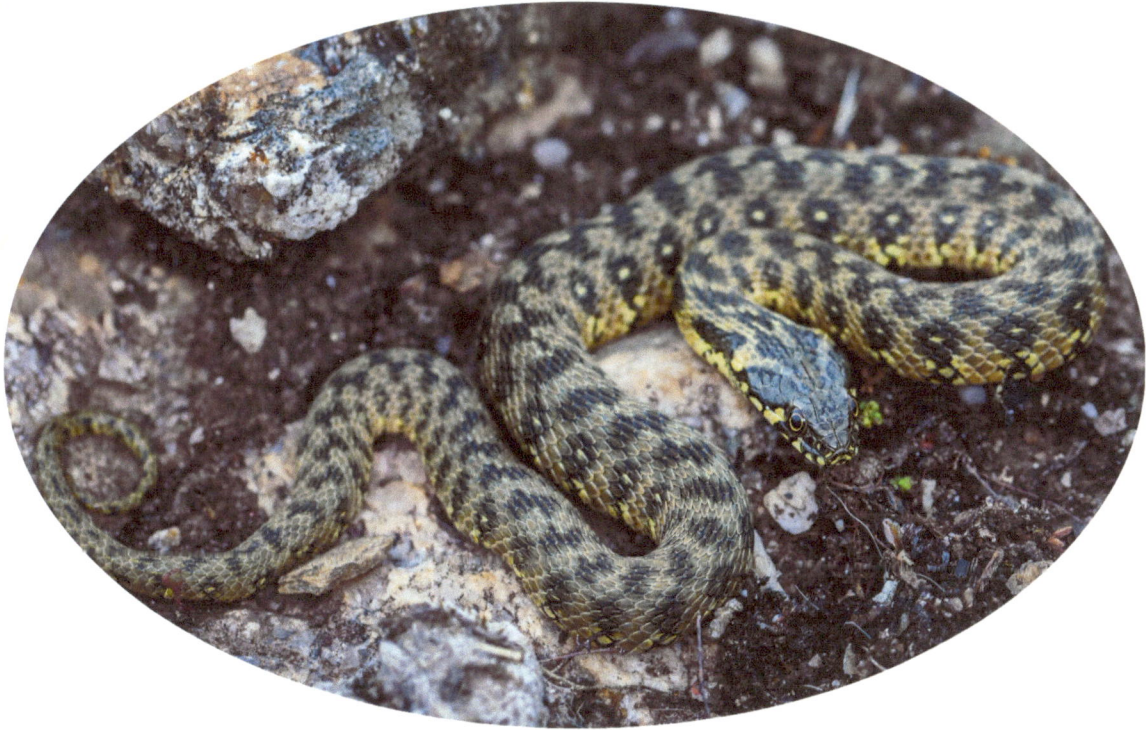

The Viperine Snake is also known as the Viperine Water Snake. The snake gets its common name because it looks like an adder, though it is not actually a viper.

W is for Western Diamondback Rattlesnake

Crotalus atrox

Western Diamondback Rattlesnakes have fangs that fold flat in their mouth when not in use. The rattle at the end of their tail is made from keratin, the same protein that helps form your hair and nails.

X is for *Xenopeltis unicolor*

Xenopeltis unicolor

<u>Xenopeltis unicolor</u> is commonly called the Sunbeam Snake. These snakes have iridescent scales—this means they shine in the light.

Y is for Yellow-bellied Sea Snake

Hydrophis platurus

Yellow-bellied Sea Snakes have tails shaped like paddles. They spend most of their lives in the sea.

Z is for Zebra Cobra

Naja nigricincta

The Zebra Cobra is sometimes called the Zebra Spitting Cobra or the Zebra Snake. This type of cobra can force venom out of its fangs!

29

5 Snake Facts

1 Snakes are "cold-blooded"—this means they rely on the environment to control their body temperature.

2 Snakes don't have eyelids that move!

3 Snakes smell with their tongues.

4 Snakes swallow their meal whole.

5 Snakes are found on every continent except Antartica.

Jessica Lee Anderson is an award-winning author of over 50 books for young readers. She writes snake-positive stories including the NAOMI NASH chapter book series. Jessica lives near Austin, Texas with her daughter, Ava, and husband, Michael. They have a pet corn snake named Ari they watched hatch from an egg. You can learn more about Jessica by visiting www.jessicaleeanderson.com.

Check out these other books:

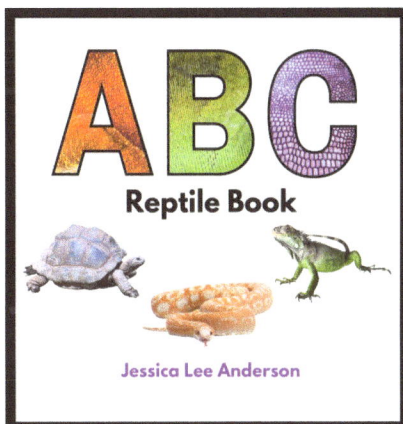

ABC
Reptile Book

Jessica Lee Anderson

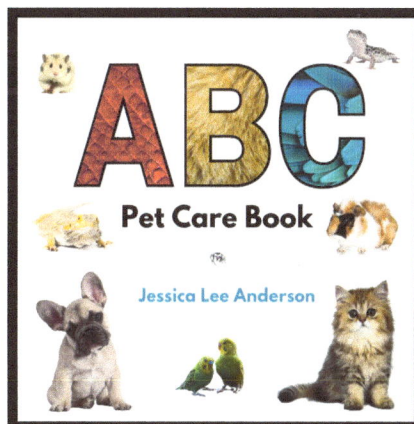

ABC
Pet Care Book

Jessica Lee Anderson

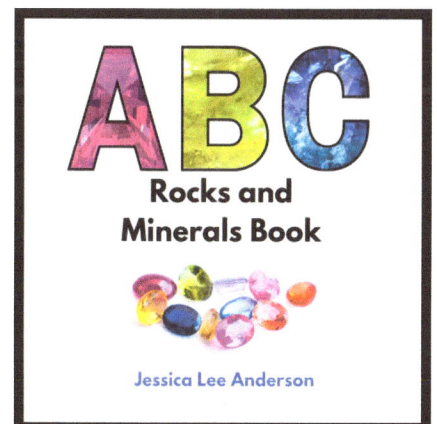

ABC
Rocks and Minerals Book

Jessica Lee Anderson

www.ingramcontent.com/pod-product-compliance
Lightning Source LLC
Chambersburg PA
CBHW061150030426
42335CB00003B/168